OTHER SIDE OF OCEAN

OTHER SIDE OF OCEAN

XIAOQIU QIU

MARSH HAWK PRESS
East Rockaway, New York·2025

Marsh Hawk books are published by Marsh Hawk Press, Inc., a not-for-profit corporation under section 501(c)3 United States Internal Revenue Code.

Book Design: Susan Quasha
FIRST EDITION

Library of Congress Cataloging-in-Publication Data
Names: Qiu, Xiaoqiu, 1992- author.
Title: Other side of ocean / Xiaoqiu Qiu.
Description: First edition. | East Rockaway, New York: Marsh Hawk Press, 2025.
Identifiers: LCCN 2024028635 | ISBN 9798987617755 (paperback)
Subjects: LCGFT: Poetry.
Classification: LCC PS3617.I88 O74 2025 | DDC 811/.6--dc23/eng/20240923
LC record available at https://lccn.loc.gov/2024028635

Contents

PART ONE: SAILS

PART TWO: WAVES

Part Three: Tides

Part Four: Shores

"[The poem] holds no mirror up to nature but…become[s] 'nature' *–continuing* 'its' marvels."

—William Carlos Williams, *Spring and All*

"A true noun, an isolated thing, does not exist in nature. Things are only the terminal points, or rather the meeting points of actions, cross-sections cut through actions, snap-shots… and the Chinese characters tend to represent them."

—Ernest Fenollosa, *The Chinese Written Character as a Medium for Poetry*

"Only, in turning pages of all this, a great sutra / I have forgotten the way home."

—Guanxiu, "In Garden of Spirit Spring", own translation

The poem written in Chinese calligraphy, with form and breath dictated by and as an extension of the landscape (Taishan, Shandong, own work)

帆
Part One: Sails

 [1]

out of Target's automatic doors
the sky is heartbreaking blue green boat thing
that a crushed coke can
tap dance
between the parking lot arrows pointing different angles
knows, this
is the edge of the world
waves of moon splashes
down its teeny tin ridges
drunk red decks
into each other
every light
of the night
tilts, I
can barely hold on
to this question,
cold wind in a desert
is from the sea:
two petals of calypso orchid
kiss tremblingly
at its lee

---

1 "Hwra", Old Chinese for "flower"

PHOTONS

If the faster I travel the slower time ticks for me, and we dreamed of one another at the opposite side of the earth. When. The book spines I carried all the way from China peeling off freshly. This morning somebody has to ask, what is your age? This particular moment will be felt old approximately two years later. Our timelines are recommended and therefore are never ours. Secretly, someone finally confesses to me at the water fountain they dream about towering mosques and fire breeding calderas they have never been to. I realize I do not miss home, I miss neverlands. I dreamt and believed the bookstore I frequented as a child will survive whatever erratic weather the planet has in store for us. I feel safe when the texts stay there no matter how much I run my fingers. To dream about a place is to wake up to a crack in time. In one of the chunky hardcovered science books I learned about photons. They travel 40,000 years to touch the blackness of our eyes at the speed of light. They themselves never age. Time stops for them. I finally went back home to China after five years and the bookstore was gone. It had been gone for ten years.

100 Pages of Proust Due on Chinese New Year's Eve

right now
I cannot bear to read
my Proust
that little
patter of
firecracker
in my phone, heels on
cobblestone
at my heart
I've to walk,
all with you
Monsieur Proust
tonight, to your signs
I am thinking
fuzzy, bunny ears
half a world away
and my nephew's finger
under the rabbit pen
their small entirety
threads in between
winter sunbeam
unaware
of my imagination
and nearly spilled
pumpkin soup
grandma brings
from the farm
snow sleeps
under a string
of footprints,
crisp and murmuring
certainty,
and each and single
of their good news!
Spring
festival lanterns,
free red tassels
dangle at the edges
of last few oranges

a sun setting,
so full
of ourselves
and the old years
still warm,
he takes
a sip, and cries
hot hot
grandma smiles
for a while,
I have lost
you, m. proust,
in your *Petit Phrase*
in your smoke-fumed room
I am thinking
Home
the other end of ocean
and what would happen
if you and i,
don't have to make
them little words
stand
for something,
and lower
their first sound,
would
the milky way be less
accidental
i open up the window
and let them all
go
at once, one
and one, and i
send them crackle
and explode
in a smoke:
com bray
bal bec
gil bert
robert
verdu

-rin,
guer-
mantes
perdu
prin-
temps
temps
temps
temps…

Gulls at Santa Monica Beach

after Louise Glück

I'm writing this poem because
someone called me old last night,

I thought about you, I come
every five years, you must know me.

one time the sun broke
all the waves made halos

I chased you with my phone
each of your steps make gold stars

each different than my dream
swallowed seconds after birth

I didn't know a single soul on that beach.

another time I came with my parents,
and took pictures

of them taking pictures. The sea, the sky,
the beach was a triptych of Gauguin,

each in their stubborn monolithic hues,
the yellow cannot see azure cannot see blue.

they were dehydrated, and don't speak a word of English.

this time, after my visa appointment, I was late,
caught between a gray sky and a dim sea

afar, the sliver of horizon lit all
red, a shooting star lay flat

it's trying to send out a message:
you will leave the time you were born

and grow into a stranger

doing not much richer, nor much worse

always you will look back over the sea
for home: it has shifted

places—but how you look out, the gull
at the slanting sun

ocean crashing by its firm, webbed feet
not sinking into sand, not an inch deep

(jiàn, "to see": an eye above a pair of feet)

Yosemite Woods

pillowing on a log in the forest
above   the swaying sky between cedars
swirls down   float
by   float
last time I looked
at the sky this way, I was with an old friend
under a bodhi tree near a lake in Fuzhou city   he told me
the last time he looked this way, he was six, on a haystack
surrounded by dirt splattered oxen.
somehow between these strikes of clocks
marked eons
so much happened
before our hearts once more become settled and hear
the wind outside   of itself.
the sun grazes my nose   every other second
I see branches entangle
the leaves   entangle
the cicada wings   entangle
bird feathers   everything
is an intersection, and memories—
only when you re-member them, starts to stir
and whirl, and 沙(sha) 沙(sha), 沙(sha) 沙(sha)
like wind-branches, making knots
after knots
that cannot
unlock. in the quiet
of the eye, in the limits of your
inner void, you see between sounds,
holding still,
light.

Home Again

Rivers, except on my grandma's washboard
nuzzling, are pairs of spellbound eyes
to the sky

久

I met an old lady washing clothes by the river,
face familiar.
"you probably don't remember me," she told me in Wu
"but *ngo ke ngu du qi le eh"*, *I saw you grew up here*—
and I remembered
I don't remember her.

久

the paper remains of characters
                    piling up   in the blackened basin
       grandma burned   for my safe return
I try to sound them out: a wet   warmth

久

I stumbled upon a cupboard, the panel of painting was faded;
a feeling of something important, something green
sat me down:
memory docks at some obscure bank like a rusted boat
then one day, it sinks

久

I took time to count the money I packed
in red packets for my nephew, ¥688—
But he turned out already a freshman at the dinner:
If you pay back missed time with time
You end up slipping right through it

the streets grew in every direction
even when my feet touch them, there is a distance

又

even at night, the cicadas' songs from
the streets fill my room.
Nowadays the nights are warm
Enough for them to sing.
As kids, we used to chase
their songs, from tree
to tree. None of us caught
any. My grandpa brought home one
day, in a bottle. A cicada with beautiful
green wings. We kept it
all summer, it never
sang.

又

Hometown baozi tastes better than all Chinatown combined
or, is the familiar equals the better?
or are our hearts like tree trunks
only grow soft stems when cut in half

又

mother grew a habit of retelling me stories before I could remember things
she is knitting a story out of me,
while I tried my whole life to unspool self from selves, besides
when it's done, who is left there to wear it?

又

The traveler has to knock at every alien door to come to his own, says Tagore
I have knocked on the alien doors
Now my own is one, too.

(又 yòu, "again" or used to indicate different iterations of the same title in Classical Chinese poems)

Untitled Landscapes: Shanghai

At stoplights, how we stand apart agrees to a silence
The wind lashes in between sounds it all out word for word

The escalators at metro exits are always narrow, single-filed
After wearing so much of each other's gaze for the day, levitate

In place the sun cannot reach, the bright colors of an alley opens narrowly to the main street
The eyes of passers-by have pecked it clean

The colorful clothes on the high apartment balconies
Diverse pupils that never see one another

Stars are dim in nightsky.
Though not because the city lights are too bright
But that too few remembers to look up from their screen lights

Might as well put away the umbrella, the thin rains stroke from the sides
Determined to pry the child in me out

I missed the bus, now there are only scraps of people's heart at the stop
scavenged ravenously by a homeless wind

Every day, question of existence lies in the center of the square like a giant ice sculp
People passing by take selfies in front of it, using only portrait mode

沪 沪 沪 沪 沪 沪 沪

Untitled Landscapes: Cuba

all morning, he walked straight, cut open several *santería* singings, spilled them over the squares
and fed his rationed bread to a puppy in front of a blue trashcan

do', tre', sei', die', lo' santo' y cri'to
leaving out the s to help the surfs keep their beat

dim lamps flicker the slim gravel road.
The night cannot close. Nor can we enter it.

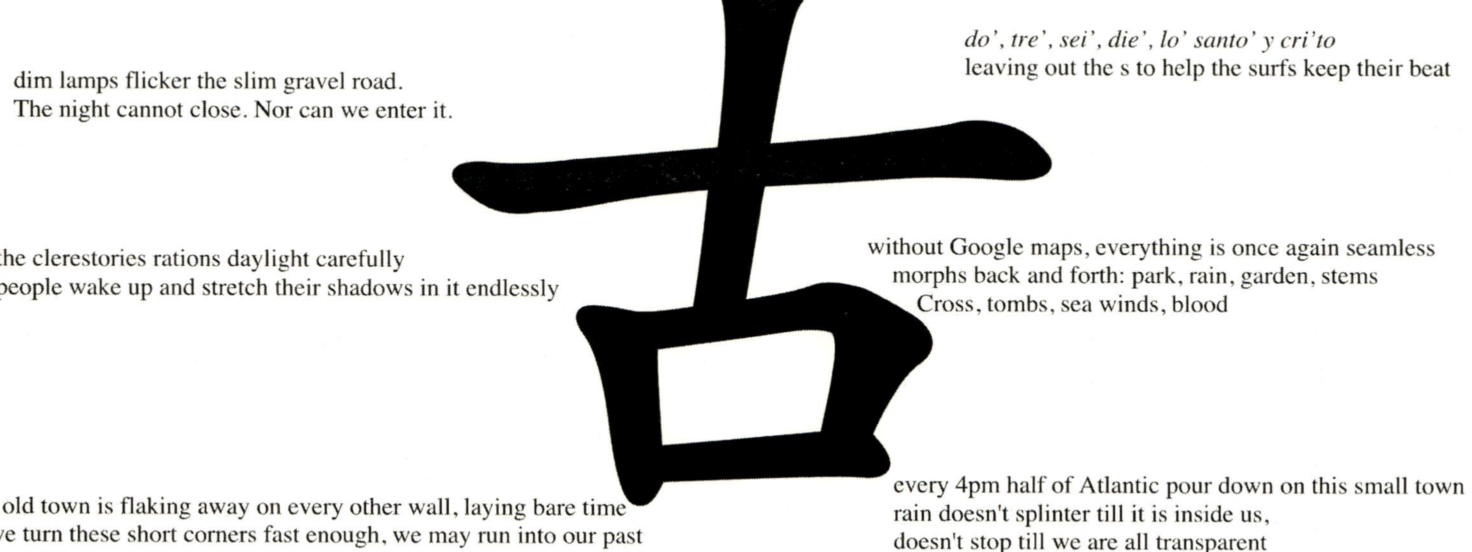

without Google maps, everything is once again seamless
morphs back and forth: park, rain, garden, stems
Cross, tombs, sea winds, blood

the clerestories rations daylight carefully
people wake up and stretch their shadows in it endlessly

every 4pm half of Atlantic pour down on this small town
rain doesn't splinter till it is inside us,
doesn't stop till we are all transparent

the old town is flaking away on every other wall, laying bare time
if we turn these short corners fast enough, we may run into our past

(古 gu: abbreviation for "Cuba" in Chinese, meaning "ancient")

Purpose of Visit

Because a past me is not apparitional enough for me to write about, I keep folding inward until my shadows stretch across the sea and lie like a seed placeholding as an object of grief. This provides temporary proof to an ancient dichotomy between roots and belonging. I came here alone. Only a California thrasher gets trapped inside an airport, we feel its always frantic colors. Every piece of dome promises a sky but none gives the blue exit. I realize these endless walls are not young. Outside, a plague scrapes the traffic clean and exposes marigolds' dream from a highway's seams. I begin to see how I got here. As a kid, my mom encouraged me to use my hands to aid my speech as if words are better felt on fingertips. I held up my palms as walls to every morning mist to listen to their secrets. They cut across me like first daydreams. Any documentation required in life presupposes small cuts on your skin, as you fit your uneven, love-beaten torso through its rectangular blanks. All knives are cast by another knife and therefore are never whole. I almost re-member them. When my dad brought a basket of peeled mikans to see me in boarding school, I had made a difference between interior confession, which was the bloodred shadows of dry snail shells impressed upon the evening school walls, and an exterior one. The skills to fold, however, gives such an impenetrable disguise that the inside of the paper is never a question of the origami, once you have decided which self to fold against. I at this did not tell my dad the night before I had a knife on my neck. It was about the same tem-perature as a pen. I was an easy target as they thought I was mute and couldn't write. At the same time, if you come over to the other side of the skin, you will see the writing grow. When asked to sign, I realize I have never written my name in front of myself. Unlike truth, secrets are told pretty much the same shape to someone else. Still only one side of them tingles. When they do, they do so like mountains. Other students pretended to pass by, as I cried sheets and sheets of rice papers on the second calligraphy class. It haloed the ink and therefore footprints on soft snows. All rituals are private in nature. It is okay. The depth is from heart to hand, not the front and back of paper. Somethings just can't be told in Chinese. The only certain thing you know is the wound. I'm afraid to go out today because I can't

心 "xīn": heart

必 "bì", certainty: a laceration over the heart

宓 "mì", silence: a rooftop (home) over this certainty

密 "mì", secret: a lacerated heart

hide everything under my mask. The same knifing looks. So I stop a second more at traffic lights. We let our past run ahead but they always turn back to hold our hands. Lead on. I rode behind my dad's bike to move to the city. I and all the grasshoppers I took with me in the bottle knew I love. By moving them away I killed them. I begin to see the rationales of mass extinctions. I have no contacts in this next world. If only regrowth depends on perishability. The coil of rain. The angle of clouds. The rustle of dirt. My wounds have grown like a wall. I have raised them like a child. In this foreign country, they are the only family I know. These are my dependents. My timid self crouching like a riverbed before you. My tormented self giving way like windslices behind you. I thought I got good at killing. The knife grows glows growls inside me and I am wielding it willing it to undivide me. That, it cannot do. Running away equals running into. Here goes an ocean. Here goes a decade. Here I am. On the inside, the laceration of the wound is visible on the dome like a milky way, a billion trapped stars, glittering from horizon to horizon, imagine all the colors you have never seen before. The secret is you can't heal a wound that grows. Except, folding your legs against the universe. Say, thanks for inviting. I am going home.

Terrace of Machu Picchu

The world does not turn
 dark
   We turn our gaze down to the underworld
  at night
        Stars open light
          at the other end

The mists do not move
  They stop to let the rinsed sunrays
 fall
      back to the wet stones
        Their lost frames of gold

They built a church above a *wak'a*
    it's shaken loose in earthquakes, and people
circumvent:
      I traveled oceans with my ruins
  here
        trailing behind me
    still
          I was told there were two
    in each:
          One *wak'a* to create, one to destroy
              The conquistadors and I
        buried
                only one half of the past
                  and let loose the other

I don't have enough emotion for all the mountains
    the stone collapsed onto another
      through the openings of wreckage, love is
  tangible

---

the mind shapes the land before it
was a landscape, it was never a land, it was
a place-mind,
wrapped in a mind-place, the concussive, in-spreading
of a gravity,
falling from branch to branch, the unclattering
of thoughts with boundaries, the parallel seeing, looked as
well as looking, smooth stones pelt from light to light, when
impressed upon, presses as an embrace, a
sprout-out-of-earth, opens while closes
the land, the poet tears apart and soils
their own eyes
into the scape as any other
rainwater

Lime around Seine

I've only now noticed it was charged
in euros, my Lime pass, and that in the front basket
the empty bag of ficelle and an azure umbrella,
makes my heart fall out when
I see someone's poem about
past is irretrievably present

Noon tides up the plane tree shadows
drop them soft sprinkles of gravels
rise, I go up, up, washing my face in
and out their freckled silence, the bikes, the strollers,
the light denim pants, in and out, the shades, and in
the Eiffels back and forth in the hands of peddlers,
the chevalier's fingers gilded over onto the next
each entangles a lateness a second ago

—simply, *j'arrive*
the time that is a place when in third grade
Wednesday afternoon school ends early at 3,
teachers gather us at the hall, portraits of Gorky and Mao,
in 90's China
it could have been, "*depechez-vous, les enfants*!"
I'm blanking on the exact words,
and we start to pedal, home is over a bridge
Au-Bau never takes down his earbuds,
Yan-Yan has a loud sneeze
and Chinese plane trees, *vuton*, have leaves shape of our palms
their shadows spindly brush past our cheeks:
dark, light, dark, light
in the pedal, pedal, pedal, conducting our singing:

"Cet air qui m'obsède jour et nuit
Cet air n'est pas né d'aujourd'hui
Il vient d'aussi loin que je viens
Traîné par cent mille musiciens"

I saw Au-Bau just now in the crowd, in front of stoplights on Cours-la-Reine—
I had seen him in Shanghai, 29th floor, but I couldn't see him, his
white shirt and black tie—*mais si, c'est lui*! I know those eyes!
That one,   next to the   police car,   blue scooter,   black dress,   AirPods,   bra
showing   a little,   the way   she folds   her neck   so slightly   over   shoulder
the afternoon cloud   leans on   another,   forgets to   move
the wind,   the music,   the eyes,
the city
they're not born here today, they come as far as I have come.

the Airbnb host teaches at Sorbonne, and has a bookshelf of Emil
Cioran, in new and dusted, *being born was a catastrophe*, he says,
a fact survivors try to flee from. and the Seine under Eiffel continues
to smell like pisspots and fish scales when I walk towards it, and the sun continues
to knead gold waves behind me when I walk past it, in secret, as the past second
had just exiled this one, as birth has exiled us when we were born,
as we turn,   for a home,
and catch   some shards   of halos   in our iris,   and turn back,
wonder which darkened stair we had just descended from,   bleeding

Mother

"Qual io fui vivo, tal son morto" –Inferno

My mother never tells me how she almost died giving birth to me. When I'm back in the US and am handed the snake plant I asked someone to sit over the summer, I tilt my head at how it is more dead and alive. As far away, her voice fades, and I hear the softer parts clearer. As the desiccated leaves all hoist up skyward, tips lower only at the last curl. The green tautened by pale veins, pulling horizontal, immovable. I realize when on display, we both perform our liveliness as *nature morte*. Still life. I still see my lifelong high school friends. They smile more vividly than ever in their Stories. Sooner or later they freeze. All things are re-membered today. They are only seamless under the strokes of our fingers. In Musée D'Orsay I watched Monet flick his coagulated strokes in a portrait of his dying wife. Each thin, sharp lines attack Camille's cheeks with more merciless passion. They stop right there. Her face living as far as her dying. Our living cells kill themselves every second. When they leave our bodies, we carefully vacuum them and bag them away and impersonate a clean visage that consciousness is an uninterrupted stream of self. The day before my flight across the Pacific, Dad drove us by the old ward where Mom was admitted. She crooned under my ear finally: "I wasn't thinking about how I was going to die before I gave birth to you. I thought about how you will give birth to a mother after you are born."

(In Oracle Bone Script, the character of "death" 死 resembles a mother nursing a child)

Sunflowers in Soup

"Kveld lifir maðr ekki
Eptir kvið norna."
("A man does not live a single evening
After the decree of the fates.") –Poetic Edda

In that moment, you're
naked: it did not
present, but disguise
Stroke
after color-
ful stroke, it is always
half and more
than what it stems:
the dying cannot commiserate
the guilt of the dead;
they have their own decay, petal
after petal, to hide behind.
only in the rich, spontaneous cata-
strophe, death becomes meta-
phoric, the tawny seed beds discharge
A dark remorse
of the kneeling figure: the vividness
of it, the dying laid level
with the dead, the discoloring backdrops—
this has always been the painting
Every day, when death comes
with its pre-sketched yellow edges, you
the leaf that grows beside
it, no less bright and full enough
to fall.

亡: to perish

Velociraptor

I dread having kids.
Every time I go back to China I see my friends' kids grow up leapfroggingly like evolutions of Pokémon.
"*geh me nyie zy lo*"
That's what you get for living abroad, mom says, *like living in fay time*
when you go back to the realm of human, you get run over by time speeding.
I watch the lips of my cousin's 2-year-old push away a spoon of stinky tofu in slow motion like a truck backing a foldable *no parking* sign. Then he cries.
I remember watching my cousin cry the same way as a baby last time I was in China (I swear).
But where do they all go while I was gone? I ask mom, *time must go somewhere*.
Like behind a magical curtain where they hide & hold
their laugh till their cheeks grown pomegranate red
at our insouciance of missing their exposing ankles.
Like Proust reminds us in Celtic myth the past is hidden
outside this realm beyond our intellect
in some hidden objects
encountered only by pure chance.
Every social media wants
to recommend me X years ago
on this day every day these are not
by pure chance
the past must not be in those objects.
I scrambled to bring a gift to my friend in China to thank him
for still hanging out with me after all these years
most of which I'm not there.
I picked up a velociraptor toy at
a local Target. It had beautiful feathers of aquamarine
and emerald green reminds me of the summer
soccer field we used to sleep on as kids
& watch a giant plane fly over our heads
& imagine its shadow on our face a prehistoric pterosaur
& our hairs blew like wind forgot to leave.
I don't think he is still into dinosaurs like me but maybe his daughter would like it?
At the dinner his face budded like autumn chrysanthemum, and flapped his fingers over his daughter's puffy dimple like a pair of wings
Thank you for the dinosaur. I love it.
Thank you for always reminding me of the kid in me.

Flower Duet from Walgreens at Midnight

("and they play it so loud so that the homeless can't sleep there")

the thick dome of night.

that we can't breathe in it

makes it   the sea

and so   are the pair of car lights

opens

and closes

and closes

and opens

through the lamp poles

bioluminescent

we're barred from their conversations

a cloud cumulus is only *told*

apart from a cirrus

they are more   pothos whose

untrimmed fingers sign two   words

a day

close and

open,   like

jellyfish

some times along E. Flamingo Rd.

a music stops and a shop opens

the old mesquite tree next to a smaller road

blooms, plastic bags, bottles, gravels:

people kick them around like their dried

hellos

a moment and

the cars and jets charge through

Saturday noon, pieces of scorching sun

pelt away on their high cold windows,

fleeing currents.

at last, she sleeps,

corner of mouth curves

the same smile as her boy in her arms
all the lights on the hills palpitates around
so sound, so worryless, a spring
I am too small to see them move.
behind the transformer station
What makes the starless sky a
whose nightblack shadow barely
dead sea, makes us
blankets their torsos:
reflections:

the magic is not there there
(the night is too contiguous to be there)

when I closes, they opens
(I alone dark petals, everywhere opens)

Feb 13th, E 57th St.

"Each petal of my heart, Each heart of its petals.
Tangling and untangling, Leaving few strands of sorrow to fall."
—Li Qingzhao

tonight, many roads in this city should
be jammed,
I hear the soft cold winds as I descend
the stairs

they have put small roses at the crevices
of the beams,
one to another in unequal distances,
looking

somewhere the streetlights come up splays
heavily the windows,
people go on breathing into
the heat with their faces

we pass each other,
you make yourself not look
at me,

my heartbreaks both ways.
I shut the door

very much behind me, and ahead
the small pinecone stands in the middle

of the road, its cruel contours
against the thin moon

Crossing Bainbridge Ferry

1

I didn't sea was there.
Against the advancing keel
The streak of cormorant's float
Cuts the Pacific in two.
Home is always at the other half.

2

Inside, I sit with sixty other people, look the same
Direction at sea, all we are we are lines on a chart,
Extend our infiniteness separately. Outside,
the wind has shrunken the sea, the gust all
surround us, on the bow, our gazes blown across
Each other. In the blipness, we as endpoints, are free

3

The pine shadows a bit bluer, deepens
The sea, to our hands, branches of sky opens
Between islands, sun behind clouds, livid sheaves
Of beams, grew my eyes
a bit brighter, the lack of contrast –
Last night, I got lost in the city
And stopped at traffic lights to look at my phone
In front of a pile of tattered sheets beside a hotel gate.
The dark wind. The dense rooflines. The city light with colors.
The homeless sat up from the sheets, and realized I did not stop for him,
Eyes dimmed, went back to measureless sleep

4

I am giving hyperreality a chance, I pretend
Home is just over the hills of these isles, that we
Are going somewhere. That before me is a life
I lived, rice fields and bamboo leaves for twenty years,
Behind me is a dream, I write and teach poetry
In a foreign tongue, plague and desert sun—
O Salish winds that entrance the whirling straits,

Folding glaciers into sculptures of songs!
O floodstream and tidal surge,
Narrow seas and Desolation Sound!
How do you know my skin when I could only
Possess it? How do you speak while my pen can
Only betray my writing? How you
Have sunken the ocean while I
Still sails, eyes unmoved,
I see strings of trees ashore, billow
To your lee, row of white cottages
Far and near, cave in
Each into each.

5

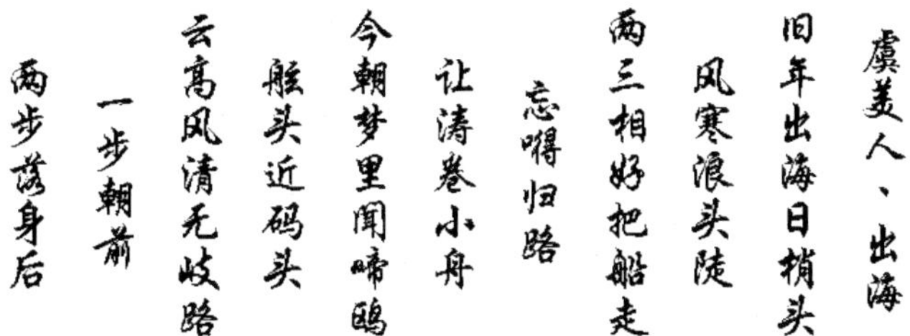

虞美人、出海

旧年出海日梢头
风寒浪头陡
两三相好把船走
忘嘚归路
让涛卷小舟
今朝梦里闻啼鸥
舷头近码头
云高风清无岐路
一步朝前
两步落身后

In the old years he goes out to sea at sun in branches
Cold wind and folds of steep tides
Two and three of them hurry aboard
Lost their way home, they
Let turbid waves swirl little boat;
Today seagulls wake him from a snooze
Bow head closes in on wharf head
Homeward after twenty autumns
High clouds, clear winds, no forked road
He lands one step ahead, and two backwards

6

Like life, we are dropped off on this small island, given
90 minutes to explore, before the next ferry comes to collect us,
Some stuff themselves into rental cars in the nearby parking lot
Driving all the way to the other side to see the big rocks, some
Have nice hotels booked, who already sent a shuttle for pickups,
Some run, cheeks taut like bowstrings, to the station for the next bus, while
You and me, empty pocketed, strolled to the nearest beach, and walked just
Far enough to see the ducks by the shore, and spent our
Last dime on poké bowls (a bit cold) in the first restaurant we saw
Now we are in the line for the ferry home, right on time
For the sun out of clouds and warm through windows

Untitled Landscapes: Las Vegas

Moon   stops   wind-leaves

the palm   shadows   move   a long   crack on

the parking lot   drunkard   on   sunroof

I am in the way.

where between the barbs, iron
pupils, angular, thinking, the crow

land projects—concave, cordon
to diagonal, trackwayed, and hard

its uneven feathers taper to a point
the sierra ridges are black, bent

it shakes its head, the machine
neck, horizontal

Five crows, each

Qualifying each

Roots

the neon billboard

Before the drizzle

Sped trackways round the

Dark jeep engine

White curb

mountains   mountains
of ink   clouds
collapse   upon
the   horizon

under   the
green   gazebo
a pigeon   peck peck
seeds

Indeed, the loud eye of the sudden moon

the clouds before sundown upon the strip
flocks of cardinal plumes
I reach for my phone—
they're scared away

"you once told me Las Vegas is no place to make home.
We were sitting on the wooden fence that invited very
little wind and a sky of blood-pink. People are al-
ways in each other's way, you said. But none of them had
a place to go. Sands didn't want to make a desert—
they are just parts of mountains that wanted to see the world,
taking a long break, from carrying winds and rains."

Woman on a High Stool, Matisse, Las Vegas

only where the shadow is
on a vaulted bank, water is black
and thin, before streams down
to the spare spaces of trash
the riverbed, it shines blue, skirted
sky against strokes of teal, half-pleated
bushes, edges hollow out, the wooden
cityscape: I don't know who she is—
but I have known them. That look. They wrap
their entire, chromatic life behind
a sweat-saturated black, and waits with
clasped hands, tinted by
some sclera-eating sun
on the strip, a tourist guy confesses
he's scared of homeless artists
singing aggressively, to TV news
cut to exterior, day, wide shot of
a group of them
unsure if should get up
on their always gray carpets, gray
that rams through their scarves, ropes,
paint-peeled banisters and the front ceramic
tiles of Caesar's Palace, and if the gray has toned
them, or they it, and
to the audience behind the frame, if
there's something they're supposed to say.

Undasein

*"The word
'Nantahala' derives
from Cherokee,
meaning 'Land of the
Noonday Sun'
because in some spots,
the sun reaches the
deep gorges of the
forest only when it is
high overhead at
midday."*

I hear the sound of sunrays today
its timbre universal, its volume almost zero

the stems grow. The flap of gossamer wings,
the strings of webs, throb rainbow, rainbow—

the echo of it, splashes every branch, every vine
if you slow your heart enough, you hear

when you listen, you hear their attentive
listening, too. For once, a leaf detaches,

swings and turns in winds, and caught
on a web, and wiggles with its tiny edges

to the wind, like a toetip bobbing
to music: that it can't control it

gives it freedom. All around me
leaf shadows punctured by lights

red and yellow, the dead stalks, ebb
and flow: I never realize how much death

is around me—I find nothing
cruel. The expressive, extricating

enflame of death: the protagonist
to "environment": that which surrounds.

All these leaves attached to the branch, what
if life is not being, not existing—I

am that which surrounds. The greenness of leaves
being never now-here—except at noon,

I see my shadow fold, like a petal,
and the buzz of a wasp, speed on its road

Etymology Studies

屋*home* equals 尸 *drapery cloth* and 至 *arrow stuck in the ground*;
only when I lift up the curtains, do I see home is a dead end

In 苦 *bitter and suffering*, neither the 艸*grass* nor the 口*mouth* produces bitterness; it is what lies 十*in between*. Suffering is existential, not essential.

圍 is to *surround, encircle*;
claustrophobic is when you put your hands against the walls and miss the window at the heart.

名 name is 月*crescent moon* and 口*mouth*; we only call them out at dark to identify each other.
In daytime, we always know ourselves; we are allowed half of our lives to wonder who we are.

樂 *happiness*:
I found a clover with four petals!

as in *desire*: a man thinking about getting up when he is still kneeling.
Desire is your future self weighing you down.

宛: *as if/winding*
earphone cord as-ifs on my sheet, there is
no words in English for “long rivers” as in Yangtze
mountains and mountains
my arms around my kneecap

there was an ancient debate
about the meaning of “time”:
the Germanic tribes believed
time was like twigs, to make use,
one needed to cut it into equal pieces
a certitude ensuring its functionality,
hence “time” and “*zeit*” from “*deh-imo*”,
“to divide”;
the Romance tribes thought
the opposite, time was already
broken, like pearls on a riverbed,
and needed to be stringed, concatenated,
into a glowing whole, whence sense can flow,
hence “*temps*” and “*tiempo*” from “*tempos*”
“to string”, or “to stretch”.
Or perhaps, they were two perspectives
of the same movement—
As the Sinic tribes, drew a symbol
of hand, meaning “to grasp”
under the symbol of a foot,
or “to go”, to indicate time,
no one knows for sure what they meant—
I am guessing, however, “time” for them
is like a horse, is to be reined in,
or to gallop, hence “grasp how you are going”,
or maybe “know what lies ahead”:
Time is
how you pace the world.

Mojave

After a wettest winter

April.

Desert of real. (There is no here there.

ten thousand young tumble - weeds

wait

like a map.

A
small
stream
of
broo
k
nec
k
ing
be
t
ween

gasping –
– gagging

a green-tailed gecko
lick-lick its eyeball

snowline perches like a dead owl

A triangle roadsign
faded red edges
missingacorner
r e a ds

“\N I N D”

Untitled Landscapes: Japan

ぼう
"Bō"
could mean
:

帽 a Hat

望 Full Moon,
Observe

暮雨 Evening Rain

坊 a Boy,
a Monk

某 Someone,
Somewhere; I, Me

棒 a Bar,
a Staff

房 a Room, a Monastery

暴 Violence, Illegality, Unreasonableness

貌 Appearance, Complexion; Shape and Form

Hence,

The Monk Boy

Somewhere above his hat,

Evening rains, the complexions of

Him, full moons/ observes,

A violence/ an illegality,

his own broom sweeps

The room/ the monastery,

The only other sound.

Untitled Landscapes: Rome

Evening symphony
at the Coliseum
the conductor
and his hands.
The flock of birds above
dashes
and turns, in one
without lead
and without end

the

clouds

behind the

Aqueduct arches:

freed once

from the blue

of the

sky.

this city is made
of frames:
passing through
each, will teach
you time
is manmade

the evening beats
on Tuscan windows
like a drunkard,
fingers all red:
I let him in
all the way to the bar

a single clover
at the crevice
holds the pillar
and the square
from collapsing
into a new street

(罗 luo: first character of 罗马, "Rome" in Chinese,
meaning "to display")

波

Part Two: Waves

Family Outing in Piedmont Park

ripples   mallard wing   percuss

percuss

on,   "those little lip rings on the museum glass, kids

never cease to play…"

winds below   swing

bank leaves, stubble   green bushes itchy

cheeks

the African boy   unwraps   his popsicle

with mommy's fingers   overlap the cream

falls   the meadow   sky

a slope   all the clouds

spritzing apart   –

"those Kongo dancing masks   with long beaks

I swear I'd see them   in a dream,   the first one

I ever had…"

a duck's first feet   on last palmful of spring

soil,   grandpa's   playful push

light   on the swing: suddenly everyone laughs,

uncurdling the Atlanta skylines   a cursive

under sun   like wind-writ   mulberry branch

from the other side of the sea—

they don't plant those trees here;

and the mallards took flight

wetting our hairs

I recognize my smile among theirs, far

from home,

we are from each other's dream

(夢mèng, dream)

Vindhyachal

Even now
this hill tucks
the horizon away
and carries the sun
on its shoulder
the small red houses
on the terraced fields
the clouds snuggle on the sky-banks
a small white road climbs
to remind
the windmill to wave
its hands
the wind carelessly
crosses
the border between Urdu
and Hindi
and translates
seeds
to a spring

Two Statues in a Farmfield in Henan

for Zhi-Zhong

he dreams a little,   I assume, sky
bright green as   summer rice fields,
or a farm, blooms of   soft-stalked stars
broken arrowheads of   wars foretold;
like the other tomb guardian,   30 meters away
bowing to him   in the selfsame posture
creviced fingers wrap around a   thumb
carved flat on surface: such humility,
how they fold together,   self-curving
like dangling lily petals   barely
join one another   under a dew;
many could have   humbled them,
many could have   brought them down—
rebels, Red Guards,   renovations.
they stood two meters tall,   locked gaze
for an entire   millennium:
people now use the edge   of the tomb's shrine
to open   wine bottles.
and it was   noon,
the hot air rose,   the green
began to dense.   and I had looked
and found no place to shade,   I saw
against the rays,   he immolates himself
into darkness, casting shadow,   and the sun
his halo,   disk of flames

Taos Mountain Diptych

In Middle English, 1399

bald / branches / branches

thaws / thwart sky / sky / skyn
【i:】

roote in the blue
【o:】

ash / ask the night awar stream / steams
【ea】 【e】

flower
【u:】

afterburn grass faces / ferns

art- i- choke green

seas yellow has slain hearte, hearte
【ɛ】 【ɛr】 【ɛr】

it blood sun / sunder
【u:】

This whirled in the the in next worlD

snow cape / cave in the horizon

toe on cloudtips

head in red clay

the only way / way

break-free \ suffocate

In Classical Nahuatl, 1399

Uncle Witsilin is busy humming. Aunt Cuicatl puts her hands up and under the sky, knitting a basket. They are born before silence. I stick my ear onto the giant rock they are leaning against. I want to see if anyone in the earth respond to their call. Their eyes do not meet. Aunt Cuicatl punctuates Uncle Witsilin with her lifting of wrist to seal each knot.

"ye maca timiquican"	*"in cuitlapilli, in atlapalli"*
"may we do not die" he sings,	"the tail, the wing" she follows,
"ye maca tipolihuican"	*"in yollohtli, in eztli"*
"may we do not perish" he sings,	"the heart, the blood" she follows,

Above, the sun gently rubs its rays on the ridges, the trail between mountains lit up all pink. People shuffle their feet between the stubbly shadows of low shrubs. Coming is corn, squash, melons and beans; going is meat, hide, horns, and bones. Around this rock, they form a circle of green and black. Each spring, Uncle takes me to see the first ice melt on the lake. I point to the fish underneath. Are they awaiting to break their voices in the new season? Are they ending to rest their bodies in the old season? Uncle arranges my bangs. He tells me a tale he picked up from the north where people built stone houses inside the cliffs. Their ancestors set out to find the Center Place to make home. Some walk above the earth. Some walk below the earth. They do not find it. They come to ask the Hummingbird, who says, "Ah! But you are walking right upon it, at some point of your life. See, the earth is a spiral."

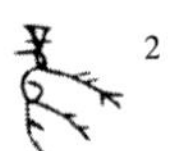 [2]

deep beneath
the canopy

a bright shadow
plunges

on a tiny leaf,
fresh, tender

a green
on the whole brown branch

every grown leaf
churns in the wind

it tilts slowly
with their beat

[2] Oracle Bone Script for 風, “wind”, pronounced “prem”

The Migrant Worker On a Train to Hangzhou

these last few hours I have settled
in the windowed sun, an empty seat
away, the little girl curls up
in my shade, cheeks crumpled up
on her little arm, red were
the tomatoes in distant farms, I can tell
her father's cotton jacket, charcoal and cheap,
unnerved by something city-y
in the coach, all the important leather shoes,
into the aisle they protrude, how polished
and refractive, their glistening smiles
loud on business video calls, I thought
about how light never penetrates things, never
self-multiplying
and the speed of train has sent the world slanting
into wafts and whorls of bleeding sun, how
our hearts are born in darkness, color
only given when they open, and I asked
if he wants his girl to sleep
on the sunsprinkled seat,
he smiled, shaking his head, and slowly
rubbed her forehead, which sunk
deeper
into his sleeves.

Old Havana Wall

above
empty cartons
and cans
black and bold
:

¡NO Arrojar Escombros!

delegado p.p.
P.N.R
C.D.R

all about the broken
bricks, bags, bottles
scrawls
blacksprays:

a/b
2+2=~~5~~
4!
re__ íon*!*
¡sí _e pue__ !

the dark, fresh, stuff
of

it
rains again
the flower drooling
pink
on the blackbin

a heart
pounding
and pounding

it rains heavier

Biking in a Heatwave Near Aix

I did get up early and get out
before the heat hit 100, yet forgot
to put on the bike battery, as it was dark
and cold as the cellar it's in, now I am
dragging the old metal uphill road, the sun
punctures my soaked back, stirring within
the syrup I had this morning (I'd bought it
thinking it was juice) as I pedal, and ped-
-al, *Ay*! to my left, the pastures all squeeze
under the parasol tree shadow, their small flowers
reach, nearly touch, the dangling branch, each
against the low white cottages peeking, light
by light, as far as the tiny village I left
behind, I had a feeling that I was born there last
night, and right now, the smooth surfs of green
hills lay down the right side, the vineyards, stake
after stake, all stand guard its round shadow, until
a red flower on the first row and last petal, and my road
parts two ways   at an aleppo pine,
I ride no more—that way, to the east, a moment the
Italian bikers will come swooshing down, necks
straight like an arrow, having beaten each gravel
and scattered all the dry leaves, leaving
the fallen berry still uncrushed, to the middle;
to the west, the food trucks from Aix, with wind
behind the yellow cart, the larks entwine their chiseled
shadows and tunes, still the same death spelled
as love, after seven centuries, the Troubadours, and it will
be so, as the truck have made it
over the top, it honks two times as it goes down
interrupting its own radio songs— yesterday it's
Johny Tu N'es Pas Un Ange, today maybe *Tien V'la Un Marin*.
There is   a blue weedhoe   aside the road
akimbo a haystack   under all of the sky, it seems more certain
now, somewhere behind it
is where I will one day die—
and the bee, upon my whiff of standing up
disturb the lavender blades, circles,
and circles back,

does she also suddenly remember
everything we do
is to forget
that we are alive?

Ann Arbor White

you didn't venmo me the pho
we had together, this spring
gets away being steamily cold
for whole three months, I blamed
the hard seedcoats that buxom its way
out of white almond flowers, you are rain
for sticking in the middle of my poems, where I want to say
I like you a lot lot, it keeps me sprouting
concealed metaphors, like a boy
practices saying "take my hand" to fallen ivies, or
to the red bricked wall, where green verges
at the fingerpresses of shadows
patter branches,
you and the afternoon sun how always progresses:
I have to keep guessing what I did wrong—
Should let images stay
objects, a second too long,
the last two sections of a paper open
for the plastic bags swivel
into ballet, the tiny raindrop crouches
on the window, in case the small wind
tapping for it to punctuate,
and the quivering snowdrop petals
I skip, like moth
when I come everything to see you, running
into me tell me you want to
make
that lunch on the last day of spring
our first date

Reading Sutras

I step on each beach in O‘ahu
But couldn’t see the sea
Over the sky and beach
Until I see it in a museum
A painting by one almost-blind
One color, central blue, muffled, materializing
End to end

至 Supreme
Speech 言
去 Rid of
Speech 言
以 Use
Hand 手
指 Point
Moon 月

I see her, violet dress, from the corner of my eye
at the ancient Elam reliefs, six god or god king figures
cut into sections of dense clay, glazed in impenetrable cuneiforms
her transparent, live, slow-dissolving pretty
I dare not turn my head
she goes up to see the Roman statues
I go down to the mummies
It drizzled in Paris outside
darkness, nearsighted, bumped from shoulder to shoulder
the exiting crowd through the mall
rainstrings down a dry, uneven stalk
ten thousand people visited Louvre each summer day

I looked up, and caught, there, top of her violet dress, her eyes
a second late:
surprised, bashful, already looking away

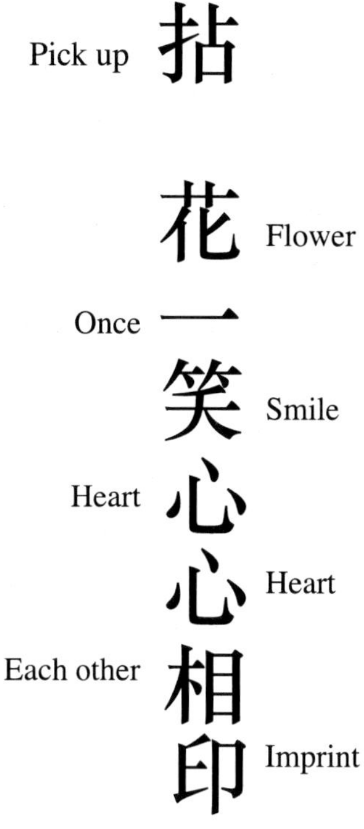

when I finally have to get on Zoom to talk to my professor,
I have just exhausted all means possible to unclog my toilet, she says:
thank you for sending me your poem, gosh
the mechanic worked all morning my skull was about to crack
and, *then I read your poem*
I realized, thank god, there is a whole world out there
It was four lines. And now the toilet the fifth.

When I open the door
the outside was quieter
than my thoughts
Humans are such noisy creatures
And as if
The woods have been listening
My heart stops
to listen, too
And there I see
some tiny stars
just between branches
and there it was
Never left
The universe.

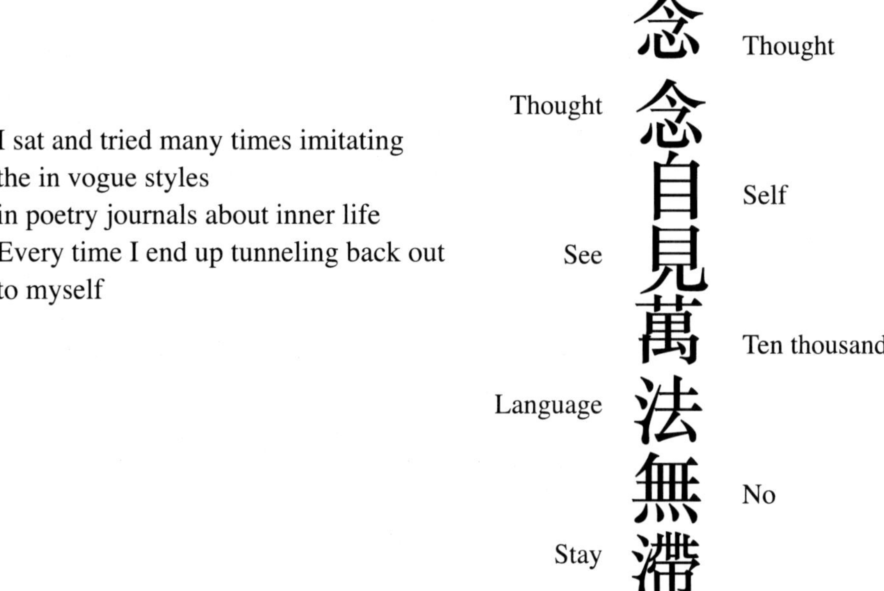

I sat and tried many times imitating
the in vogue styles
in poetry journals about inner life
Every time I end up tunneling back out
to myself

Sitting on a bench waiting for a friend to pick me up for a movie,
I believe it is possible I'm alone the majority of my life.
This foreign country, large wheels keep spinning over a narrow road,
A red plastic bag clings on to an unplanned mesquite tree.
A familiar car pulls over. Do they know me?
Half of the village I was born in does not recognize me.
I lean in. Not my friend. *I'm sorry*. I say.
That's ok, She says.
Neon flickers. Her smile superimposed on my face on the car window.
Loneliness is always a reflection.

[this sweet little word]

"Doch unsere Liebe/ heißt sie nicht Tristan
und - Isolde?/Dies süße Wörtlein: und
was es bindet/ der Liebe Bund"
—Richard Wagner

This reed stalks in my hand, bends
still
like
the thousands of others
I did not pick, on the bank, the
grey
sands
the long river ends
the mist, bird
shadows
the strands, the stones wait
and dies
in the white. I think

about the long voice messages
my mom sends me, the concerns
that ask no reply, the message bubbles one
and the next, the space in between, the long river, the
sea, and the drizzle starts, the each duck and
every rainstring, adjacent to another.

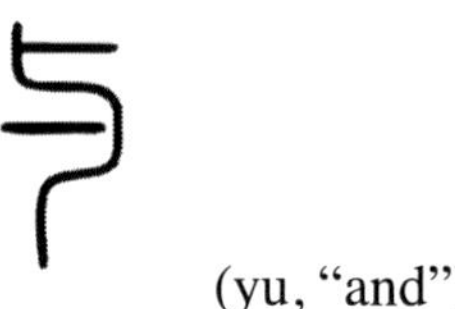

(yu, "and")

潮

Part Three: Tides

The Lady on the Porcelain in a Shumai Shop

After Miss Mo

when the chopsticks rested, the vase
is there, out of the hot steam
a painted lady, leaning in the middle, arms
on a silk mat, like a pheasant, other
hand pluck the bonsai leaves, so
content her eyes, you'd think war
has ended for last time, below
chrysanthemums spatter, her
wavy dress, cyan the entire porcelain
and in between, almost invisible
a pair of bound, atrophied feet—
the muffled, pain
of deep boudoir, glazed
for display on the dining
table:
people throw
toothpicks in it

6th of Dec, UNLV [3]

For Ahmed
Who told me, "Nothing will change if none of us starts to change."

in winter, there will be yew leaves on the pavement
between student union and BEH, freshly fallen

they are not light-weighted, in fact, in the hurry
ing boots, shoes, and scooters, they scatter not —

instead, most of them are crushed, into the cement,
like pressed brush on a hard canvas

leaving their coarse shapes of living long
after their death, the end of their leaftips continued

by the greened biketracks, splattered soleprints,
elasticizing, cascading and even

connect, the strings
and strings of dark wreaths

sparkle, like a negative of night sky
no one to develop.

Friends: slow your steps, and push your bikes,
if you can bear, look up, to the thousand live leaves—

the wind picked the fullest to fall
to remind the entire tree to rustle

---

3 Campus shooting that targeted people of color.

to a friend in Shanghai quarantine

I don't know if hope
is something I have the right
to advise you
I don't know if I can still
point at the downwind seagulls and cavorting spindrifts
and tell you
look, look at them,
something profound
and nascent
is still happening
something like you
and me,
the fog encrusts the sanded beach whole
and all the pacific
muffles in a tenor of mayfly wing,
no, tomorrow
is history again,
you have to scream new screams
and cry the same cries,
with a dry throat,
film it and upload it
and hope it will outlive a mayfly dance
about how the animals are dead
and the stars will not look
but all you wanted, those
who fumble and lie down
and scatter eclairs of hope around
all you wanted was for tomorrow
to be today, mundane, uncolored
and all we complain
is still the misty rain
sticky to our fence, the catkins
like a four-year-old, clingy to our hands
instead of the bright, April winds
that squeeze the whole spring through the teeth
of barbed wires, and left
live, reality-bleeding sighs
that never reach
the other side,

the other side of the ocean
is no longer hanging beside the sun
knitting the sea into sky,
the clouds broke
into a haze
and drove its thousand pale fingertips
gritting on these iron fences
and left undried tear marks
to be like
anyone's,
the other side of truth
is no longer lies, but whispers
murmured upon ear to ear
at sunforgotten corners of stairs
taking their humble, surprise rootlets
against eyes wide like daylight
that the other side of me,
is no longer you, but words, like
I heard it's because people like you that…
that people become less than people
and tears unrecognizable as tears
that the other side of hope
is no longer despair
but a helpless chuckle, the kind
only seen in museums, where
tragedy is better in distance
yet after which, they must get on
to another food scramble tomorrow
fictional, but always, real,
I am lucky to feel
the warmth of these tears down my cheeks
and this southernmost beach
of Shanghai, where I'm quarantined, with a city
shrouded in white
all behind,
when you said: "I don't have the luxury
to hope, but you—
you go, write your lines,
someone out there still
needs something as opaque
and as sparkling
as a poem."

into lockdowned Shanghai on the only bus

After, I didn't recognize
what they were
gesturing, but the roadside tree

branches

sway passionately under the

wind

beyond taut, jagged
curbside bushes,
rows upon rows
of yellowish green, summer fields

wavecrash

upon old rooftops
of grey and

black

all gone
into the hard, concrete asphalt
the cracked, bare distance
of an entire city

before the mute glass windows

Portland, Mr. Li

"Heaven has eyes." –Mr. Li

he sees me through the art museum glass windows
before I see him. Legs tremble in the mute wind, hollow
like his crack pipe,
hands bony, fluted Roman pillars.
I exit, open Google map, let the world
ironed out into 2D symbols, essence laid flat
with their forms, my eyes still
entangle on the edges of his dark clothes
on white marble steps,
I see my friend's text:
"they deleted my poems about the late Mr. Li,
I don't know what to do to avoid censorship."
The last conceit left in life seems to be life itself.
Then I look up and caught by eyes of the homeless man
taking aim like gun barrels
tongues wound up like trigger:
they make no meaning at me—
I cannot delete them.

Worldtree on National Road

three, green, and leaves,
converge under the
eastern slope
of a Cahokian pebble
it buds
and moves the skydome
a little
child comes
picks it
“Hey dad,
look what I found!
it’s a clover!”
and fumbles through
many, historysighed, leaves
behind
a sprouting
acorn, shell
under its name plate

(glyph origin
for both 世“world” and 葉“leaf”)

The 3rd Graders Go to School

How far am I from the truth?
All I have are two LED screens of opposite news
glaring like unsheathed blades,
and some broken words of a phone call
from a friend who still lives in Hong Kong.
I am two worlds away, and the
birds here sing so differently in the morn.
I can never get used to
a turquoise-colored dawn.
But every time I want to hold on
to something like a truth,
I think of them. I remember
how they marched down the narrow roads,
chilly and quiet in the early morning,
how they have to pass
four times the customs,
two in Shenzhen and two in Hong Kong,
and walk two hours straight,
just so they can make it
to the morning recitals,
their school classrooms at Kowloon.
I imagine them marching down
the burnt street,
in their snow-white uniforms
and flapping Red Scarves.
One of them got peanut butter on his dimple
the shape of a tiny star.
I imagine
tiny shoes wobbling in concert,
like dandelions barely holding on
at the softest touch of a wind;
and the colorful lunchboxes!
Teal green, navy blue,
blue, blue with stripes, yellow and red,
packed by their moms at 4 a.m.
4 is before the birds and bikes, I imagine,
before the honks and engines,
roadblocks and sirens,
chants and shouts,

locked arms and bent knees;
before the "we"s and "them"s,
and the smoked air and the startled pigeons.
Before anything.
They march from their average homes in Shenzhen,
and I imagine it is not a crucial difference
for any of them, that words
don't mean something.
The flags roaring in the wind
have an ideal to teach.
The smeared plaques on the ground
did an age wrong.
The giant strokes of characters
clinks and clanks on...
I imagine they walk on
and their feet know only
the next firm, solid ground.
I see their little but sharp eyes
waiting at red lights,
reaching for the world.
One by one, and always before
not after, a decision, they take it all in:
the colors of angry laser pointers
and of a dewed roadside rose,
equal, to their unmasked noses.
I imagine a boy would pick a rose
as they wait at the traffic, and put it
in a girl's hands, well before
they learn its name at school;
Before the redness
takes hold -- it is already safely
in her palm -- I imagine
they march on, perhaps singing
a song, knowing only half the lyrics,
a song that neither the chess-playing old man
nor the bulbar birds, nor the loudspeakers
will recognize, but can't help to hum along.
A song sung mostly out of tune, or even jarring
to some. And perhaps a hurrying figure
who rushed to the metro, I imagine,
who moved by their earnest and simple tune,

might stop, and give it a listen—
In my imagination, truth is not hard.
It does not ask you anything,
doesn't ask you to swear fealty, or be its gunman,
nor does it blockade you
or hold a grudge against other truths.
In my imagination, truth
is not far from the third graders,
infallibly every morning,
go to school.

Parasol Leaves on Urumqi Road

I don't know how they
synchronize, each
blade vibrates
toward a different angle, but
a stem stuck in the crevice once
the entire wind
is off balance —they didn't
fall, they rub their deep, complete
wings on the cement,
raise, and unraise,
stuck and unstuck,
then breaks, turns, opens wide,
and folds, kneels, and embraces tight
then lies down, eyes down, softly the
ground, necks bend, as if lips, coarsely
the ground, and one, and two
of them, only bare stems, small, quick
spins, twists, summersaults every
turn, they burn, and crackle, and woosh,
and swirl, and whizz, but break, but burn,
but grow, and grow—
until the rain, despite the rain, because the rain.

the more they lie flat
louder
they splatter
the rain

The Night Rose,

My arm desires a brilliant scar
of red and gold,
to illuminate some thousand hearts.
Against the thorns I stretch my arms,
and brand a souvenir of hope.
Springs and falls have come and passed;
The newcomers question the old:
"Is that a scab,
Or a petal of rose?"

渚

Part Four: Shores

The Little Dying

I sit alone with twenty other people in a ketch-up colored restaurant with ketch-up chairs and ketch-up counters and ketch-up on the table, attempt to feel

The moment I have no words to describe, this little town who dubbed itself as the biggest small town on Route 66, and the apocalyptic sunsets in western Arizona

White lights sprayed on the drops of the Tobasco lid, the pale of the tuna eyes on the bathroom poster, and this guy next to my table whose grey hair stuffs in his cap back "U.S.A."

My grandpa would call this *zen ya vu tang*, in his earthly Wu, "the wilds of fairies", or "the most bizarre", it took little to qualify as strange if you lived your whole life along a river

The sirloin gets a clean cut, fully dusted with colors, sprawled to all edges of the plate, and was sucked in two mouthfuls. Everything here wouldn't settle for a tad less than maximum

When my father assured me as he sprinkled his plants from the side and dipped unevenly to leave room for the sun and decay, that grandpa was gonna overcome it, I was fully convinced

On my way here, layers and layers of Permian sediments flurried on both sides of freeway, rocks red like dying stars, from an age when volcanos erupted for millennia and all life almost died

I'm just worried about my nephew in Hangzhou. He looked like a kid king with amazing extra-curricular talents and when we spoke in Wu Chinese, he replied in impeccable Mandarin

Even my old classmates when we had our rare reunion in closed quarters in chic Shanghai dumpling shops that no other table could overhear, they swallowed their Wu like hot soup

My coworker Lily sent me this beautiful green Boston Celtics themed birthday card with ivies but I later learned she added all the "r"s when teaching, and at bars, and in life, in general

Tonight I have the whole desert to myself, its ashtray skin, flammable like dry parchments, all ten libraries of them, and all these extra utensils that are way too clean

All of them, like small, strangely shaped snowflakes, itchy, but coldless, on my face, and I have nowhere to begin to mourn, when I got the message an ocean away, my grandpa is no more

I had imagined death to be a Great Dying, tears of shooting stars and cries of shattering quakes, while the sanded wind bashed its skull on this pane, unceremonious, soundless, on my end

In thirty years Wu will go extinct, the city folks say, I always wondered if I will watch it go, or am watching, or am going, step by step, it

And I stand up and starts to walk backwards, step by step, and trace every little dying along the way that proves me alive, out of the door, until the blowing sand hit my cheeks like sunrise

shēng, sunrise

night train to Tongxiang station

how many times in your life can
you ride the same train home. In
the dark all landscapes look
the same. These rice field ponds
might be lights of Vegas strip might
be star surges of milky way. They
kept the old seat format, the button
to recline is still under left wrist. How
lucky we are we are not constantly
reminded we are a child of the universe.
We only have to worry about buttons. I
used to laugh at my mom she had no
pursuit in life other than work, as she
threaded another button onto my pocket,
be safe out there, she said—I have spent a decade
in a foreign country in a foreign tongue
alone chasing shades of an artist
trying to write one best poem, now
my train is coming to a stop, and
I see a girl whisper to her phone
three words before hanging up:
I am home. —Everything in me collapses
          I never got to say that in the last ten years.

Birthday Alone

I poured three eggs onto the plate
another birthday coincided with Thanksgiving Day
except this is my thirtieth, and per my mom
my birthday on the lunar calendar also coincided today
so three eggs for three coincidences, per tradition,
I opened my kitchen door
and the two little gnats or flies, or whatchamacallit
rushing past me like children seeing presents,
they probably waited outside for the whole fifteen minutes,
while I attempted to break the shells—
they were tougher than air, some eggshell flakes,
like the darker fields of Rothko
fell into the yoke, and became quite elusive
every time I tried to scoop them up they
scatter and spurt in their fishy ways
some must've escaped
and sat through the sizzling of my pan
matter-of-factly, like this whole time my eyes
spellbound
on how a pair of my close friends from fifth grade got married
and cheated on each other just as violently how
my younger cousin's boy did cry
the exact the same way as she used to how
an innocent and inseparable friend of mine, how I cursed
and missed his innocence, stopped talking to me after
his father's suicide, and I alone at the other end
of the ocean, fifteen minutes later, watching the flies
dance and buzz, two small, solid speckles
between the churning and twisting lines
of steams, then land
soundlessly beside me, stilling the two pieces of world
divided by their wings: how
my entire lived life is smaller than this moment

(等deng, "equal": A twig carrying the wind)

The Cleaner on Zócalo

It's lunch time so she goes for a patrol under the bright shoulders pass by clamorous street like dead leaves on a river flows listless she put on her neon green suits the olive psychedelic graffiti snakehead on the lime-plastered wall of a McDonald clay-red she first walks to the lidless paper cup with a bite mark on the cusp hides a fruit fly over there the couple that dumped it still shines under the hot sun where she patiently clamps it and decants it and flattens it and makes it disappear into her waste cart meltable in the heat-bent air a Subway wrapper clings to a drainage grate like a palm in some ancient process of sinking when picked up grease and saliva climbing over her hands are obsidian tan reflecting sunrays dashes from screen to screen at the intersection heads looks down their phones with fingers swaddling it's 1:10 she swaddles away her long braids around her neck sticking down gazing quietly into the big black bin right at the center of the city if it is in the city and can be thrown away she's seen it all the colors and hues congregate in the bottom she rakes out a half-black egg carton and a plastic water bag and a warm napkin-wrapped corn stick out of it is a dead crow she flips it and lays it on top of the sorted pile beak skyward for a while and pushes her cart away from the hurrying high heels and Nikes comes a drumbeat on the square her sisters gather in Nahua attire for the Harvest Day arranging barleys and wheat ears in the shape of Sun radiating in that direction she sweeps the spotless street with a broom and makes sure no one sees when close enough she squats and gives one of the rays a little prune

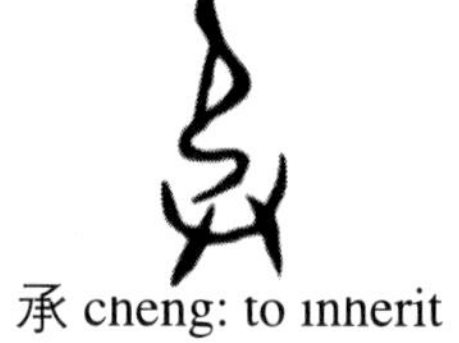

承 cheng: to inherit

Cormorant at Chicxulub Crater

Along the sun

and clouds

the cormorant drifts

up
and down

up
and down

light

and solid

like a seed,

the ocean tilts

and spilled over

a few continents:

it flaps

and drops down

a poop

Turnip

Ah-pu asks me to help her pull
the turnip out of the soil, but not with
hands, with fingers, lest the stalk may
break. We cup the silence between us
like a sakura petal: there is nothing left
to ask than the date I am leaving. The turnip
is small, its hair-like roots flail the sunny
wind as it is not his time. *Say they let you*
keep your farm, granny, would the turnip there be bigger?
I ask, the relocated chickens on the edge of roof
shadow peer back at the empty hall. *Take*
another one, she says, *I have more in the kitchen*,
the last one was undercooked a couple days ago; I
am standing on the edge of a world, and every
leaf, in the slanting autumn rays, citrines out
of their contours, flake into memories in real time,
everything's ending, I think, *this one's good*, I say,
a farmer in a distant field beats and beats
the seedlings in hands until grandma's sickle
falls out

Bai Juyi in Cuzco

As fellow wanderers at the edge of the world;
Meeting each other is like seeing an old friend.
–Bai Juyi, 816 A.D.

She opened the cash drawer and took
nothing out.
I told her China had changed so much, and its people.
I fear home's moved on. Outside,
the Andean rain bevel
at the sunrays, people's feet hurried like curtains.
The Chinese chef closed her eyes: *wanted to go home—*
but I am too old to get a job. Her callus on
the finger, like my grandma's, thin like future. A
guest barged in to pay, she
curtsied back verbally. *Your Spanish is good*, I said
They mock me still, she said, and, *I will*
see you next time! I walked
out to my last day of the city, the rain
thickened, the tourists plastered themselves on the Inca wall base
in colorful ponchos. When the street is made, does
the rain remember the rearranged stones?
She was addressing more than me, I supposed, as I have
ferried a bit of home across the Pacific to her, she shall
now close arms on her body like a chisel
on ashlar, and wait for another
midday drizzle. I started walking, they say every Inca trail
leads you home.

Saṃsāra

Every midsummer noon on the lunar calendar,
we'd prepare a feast, laying out on the long table,
jade bowls and bamboo chopsticks on the wood plaque
a pair,   a pair,   a pair.
I, being playful, liked to climb
onto the empty chairs. And you, *Tia Tia,*
waved your banana-leaf fan,
your bamboo stool creaked. You smiled:
Come down, Au-Siau, the ancestors are yet to
return. I asked, *if they are coming back,*
why can't I see them? And you, *Tia Tia*,
stretching out a hand against the wind,
lit up a red candle with another
flame, aflame,
Daylight's foot stretched long table.

Years passed. Daylight is shorter.
Again, the fake flowers to the side
wet your tombstone.
The fan on your stool
shivers in the wind.
I move it inside,
and place it among the chairs.
My palm is not big enough,
the candles flicker.
I lay out the bowls and chopsticks,
a pair,   a pair,   a pair,
a pair.

("Huí", to return, is not going back,
but going through a different circle.)

One thousand ways of a foxtail in Pudong New Economic Zone

一

amid twelve forty-storied apartment buildings
the only thing that bows
in the wind

二

At noon, I feel the sun
burning up my nape
and a small beetle
refuging at my feet

三

O the unsightly dirt!
they call you "industrial waste"
and plant you
under a sightly cement:
you plant me

四

under the white sun
a foxtail
sweat green

五

a beetle on cement
leaftip
is as tall
as rooftop

in sunset
every dust mote
is clean
what does the garbageman
come to glean?

evening drizzles
on the broken tires
chirping,
a flock of birds

八

these misty carlights
ponderously the
rain

九

broken bikes falling each
on each
a last one nudge
my back

十

and the plain pale pang pounding pile driver

百

"What was the question?"
"A crack on the cement."

千

the   ocean   winds
listens   the
waves
listen   me

Acknowledgements

I want to thank the editors and publications in which some of these poems have first appeared:

Colorado Review, Gulf Coast Journal, Unleash Press, Waxing & Waning, North American Review, Broad River Review, Meridian, Lumina, Novus Literary Arts, Sunspot, Reed Magazine, Beyond Words Literary Magazine, Ghost City Press, Etchings Press, Bacopa Review.

Additionally, “Taos Mountain Diptych” was displayed by Rita Deanin Abbey Museum. “In Garden of Spirit Spring”, my translated poem by Guanxiu, was published by *Los Angeles Review*.

Special thanks to my parents, my late grandfather Zuhua. Also big thanks to the following individuals (in alphabetical order):

My teachers: Wendy Chen, Claudia Keelan, Donald Revell, Emily Setina, Douglas Unger, Chenghui Zhang.

My colleagues and friends: Mir, Chenyin, Zheyuan, Angelo, Areej, Mark, Alex, Sabrina, Ben & Jo, Rachel, Kailee, Zhizhong.

Thanks to John Keene for selecting my collection. Thanks to the editors at Marsh Hawk Press for publishing it.

Titles From Marsh Hawk Press

Jane Augustine *Arbor Vitae; Krazy; Night Lights; A Woman's Guide to Mountain Climbing*
Tom Beckett *~~Dipstick~~ (Diptych)*
William Benton *Light on Water*
Sigman Byrd *Under the Wanderer's Star*
Patricia Carlin: *Original Green; Quantum Jitters; Second Nature*
Claudia Carlson *The Elephant House; My Chocolate Sarcophagus; Pocket Park*
Lorna Dee Cervantes: *April on Olymbia*
Meredith Cole *Miniatures*
Jon Curley *The Installation of Fear; Hybrid Moments; Scorch Marks; Remnant Halo*
Joanne D. Dwyer *RASA*
Neil de la Flor *Almost Dorothy; An Elephant's Memory of Blizzards*
Chard deNiord *Sharp Golden Thorn*
Sharon Dolin *Serious Pink*
Joanne Dominique Dwyer *Rasa*
Steve Fellner *Blind Date with Cavafy; The Weary World Rejoices*
Thomas Fink *Zeugma, Selected Poems & Poetic Series; Joyride; Peace Conference; Clarity and Other Poems; After Taxes; Gossip*
Thomas Fink and Maya D. Mason *A Pageant for Every Addiction*
Norman Finkelstein *Inside the Ghost Factory; Passing Over*
Edward Foster *A Looking-Glass for Traytors; The Beginning of Sorrows; Dire Straits; Mahrem: Things Men Should Do for Men; Sewing the Wind; What He Ought to Know*
Paolo Javier *The Feeling is Actual*
Burt Kimmelman *Abandoned Angel; Somehow; Steeple at Sunrise; Zero Point Poiesis;* with Fred Caruso *The Pond at Cape May Point*
Basil King *Disparate Beasts: Part Two; 77 Beasts; Disparate Beasts; Mirage; The Spoken Word / The Painted Hand from Learning to Draw / A History*
Martha King *Imperfect Fit*
David Lehman *The Birth of* The Best
Phillip Lopate *At the End of the Day*
Mary Mackey *Breaking the Fever; The Jaguars That Prowl Our Dreams; Sugar Zone; Travelers With No Ticket Home; Creativity*
Jason McCall *Dear Hero*
Sandy McIntosh *The After-Death History of My Mother; Between Earth and Sky; Cemetery Chess; Ernesta, in the Style of the Flamenco; Forty-Nine Guaranteed Ways to Escape Death; A Hole In the Ocean; Lesser Lights; Obsessional; Plan B.*
Stephen Paul Miller *Any Lie You Tell Will Be the Truth; The Bee Flies in May; Fort Dad; Skinny Eighth Avenue; There's Only One God and You're Not It*
Daniel Morris *Blue Poles; Bryce Passage; Hit Play; If Not for the Courage*
Gail Newman *Blood Memory*
Geoffrey O'Brien *Where Did Poetry Come From; The Blue Hill*
Sharon Olinka *The Good City*
Christina Olivares *No Map of the Earth Includes Stars*
Justin Petropoulos *Eminent Domain*
Paul Pines *Charlotte Songs; Divine Madness; Gathering Sparks; Last Call at the Tin Palace*
Jacquelyn Pope *Watermark*
George Quasha *Things Done for Themselves*
Karin Randolph *Either She Was*
Rochelle Ratner *Balancing Acts; Ben Casey Days; House and Home*
Michael Rerick *In Ways Impossible to Fold*
Corrine Robins *Facing It; One Thousand Years; Today's Menu*
Liane Strauss *The Flaws in the Story*
Eileen R. Tabios *The Inventor: A Poet's Transcolonial Autobiography; Because I Love You I Become War; The Connoisseur of Alleys; I Take Thee, English, for My Beloved; The In(ter)vention of the Hay(na)ku; The Light Sang as It Left Your Eyes; Reproductions of the Empty Flagpole; Sun Stigmata; The Thorn Rosary;* with j/j hastain *The Relational Elations of Orphaned Algebra*
Tony Trigilio: *Proof Something Happened; Craft: A Memoir*
Susan Terris *Green Leaves Unseeing; Familiar Tense; Ghost of Yesterday; Natural Defenses*
Lynne Thompson *Fretwork*
Madeline Tiger *Birds of Sorrow and Joy*
Tana Jean Welch *Latest Volcano*
Harriet Zinnes: *Drawing on the Wall; Light Light or the Curvature of the Earth; New and Selected Poems; Weather is Whether; Whither Nonstopping*
Xiaoqiu Qiu: *Other Side of Ocean*

YEAR	AUTHOR	TITLE	JUDGE
2004	Jacquelyn Pope	*Watermark*	Marie Ponsot
2005	Sigman Byrd	*Under the Wanderer's Star*	Gerald Stern
2006	Steve Fellner	*Blind Date with Cavafy*	Denise Duhamel
2007	Karin Randolph	*Either She Was*	David Shapiro
2008	Michael Rerick	*In Ways Impossible to Fold*	Thylias Moss
2009	Neil de la Flor	*Almost Dorothy*	Forrest Gander
2010	Justin Petropoulos	*Eminent Domain*	Anne Waldman
2011	Meredith Cole	*Miniatures*	Alicia Ostriker
2012	Jason McCall	*Dear Hero,*	Cornelius Eady
2013	Tom Beckett	*~~Dipstick~~ (Diptych)*	Charles Bernstein
2014	Christina Olivares	*No Map of the Earth Includes Stars*	Brenda Hillman
2015	Tana Jean Welch	*Latest Volcano*	Stephanie Strickland
2016	Robert Gibb	*After*	Mark Doty
2017	Geoffrey O'Brien	*The Blue Hill*	Meena Alexander
2018	Lynne Thompson	*Fretwork*	Jane Hirshfield
2019	Gail Newman	*Blood Memory*	Marge Piercy
2020	Tony Trigilio	*Proof Something Happened*	Susan Howe
2021	Joanne D. Dwyer	*Rasa*	David Lehman
2022	Brian Cochran	*Translation Zone*	John Yau
2023	Liane Strauss	*The Flaws in the Story*	Mary Jo Bang
2024	Xiaoqiu Qiu	*Other Side of Ocean*	John Keene